My Magnet

For a free color catalog describing Gareth Stevens' list of high-quality books, call 1-800-542-2595 (USA) or 1-800-461-9120 (Canada). Gareth Stevens' Fax: (414) 225-0377.

Library of Congress Cataloging-in-Publication Data

Pressling, Robert.
   My magnet / by Robert Pressling; photographs by Fiona Pragoff.
     p. cm. — (First step science)
   Includes bibliographical references and index.
   ISBN 0-8368-1117-8
    1. Magnets—Juvenile literature. 2. Magnets—Experiments—Juvenile literature. [1. Magnets.
  2. Magnets—Experiments. 3. Experiments.] I. Pragoff, Fiona, ill. II. Title. III. Series.
  QC757.5.P74 1994
  538—dc20
                                           94-7110

This edition first published in 1994 by
Gareth Stevens Publishing
1555 North RiverCenter Drive, Suite 201
Milwaukee, Wisconsin 53212, USA

Series editor: Patricia Lantier-Sampon
Editorial assistants: Mary Dykstra, Diane Laska
Illustrations: Mandy Doyle
Science consultant: Dr. Bryson Gore

Printed in the United States of America
1 2 3 4 5 6 7 8 9 99 98 97 96 95 94

At this time, Gareth Stevens, Inc., does not use 100 percent recycled paper, although the paper used in our books does contain about 30 percent recycled fiber. This decision was made after a careful study of current recycling procedures revealed their dubious environmental benefits. We will continue to explore recycling options.

First Step Science

My Magnet

by Robert Pressling
photographs by Fiona Pragoff

Gareth Stevens Publishing
MILWAUKEE

Look at all these objects on the refrigerator.

How do they stick there?

They have magnets on the back.

5

These magnets are different shapes and sizes.

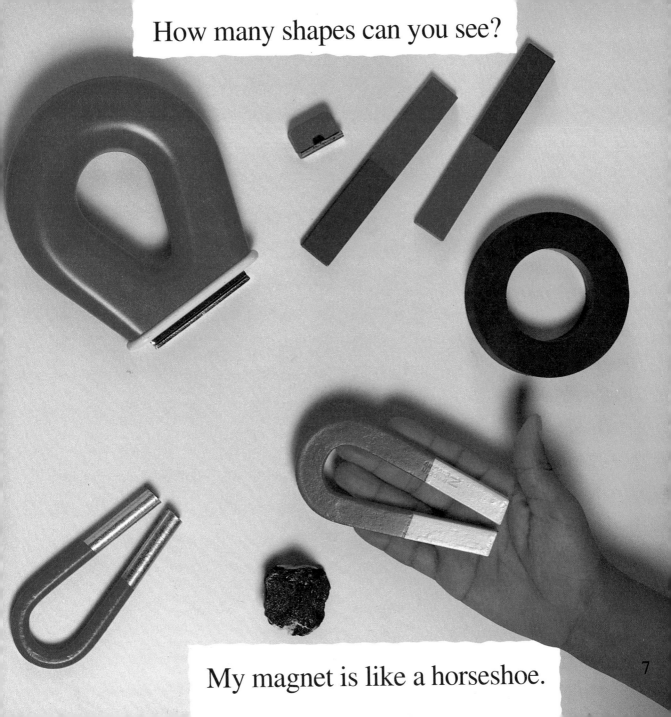

How many shapes can you see?

My magnet is like a horseshoe.

7

My magnet picks
up a spoon.

8

But it won't pick up a
toy rabbit.

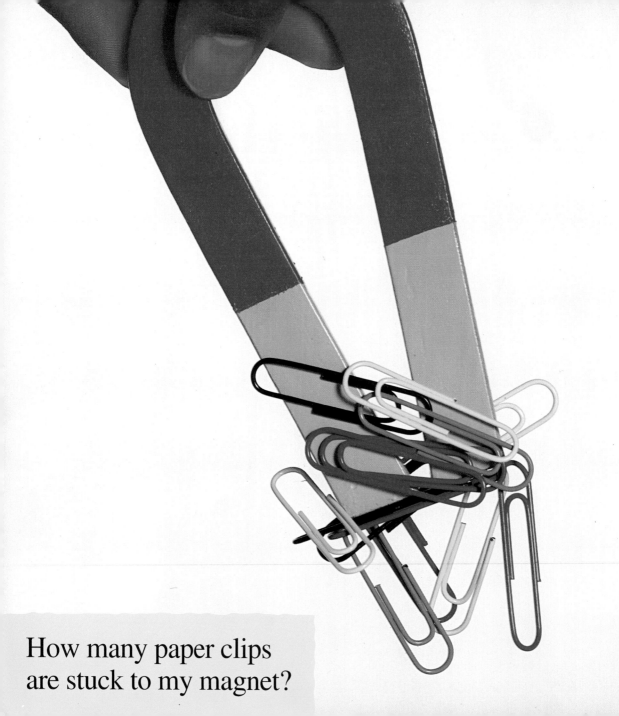

How many paper clips
are stuck to my magnet?

Georgina's magnet is stronger than mine.

11

Sometimes magnets stick together. . .

and sometimes they push apart.

We are making patterns with these iron filings.

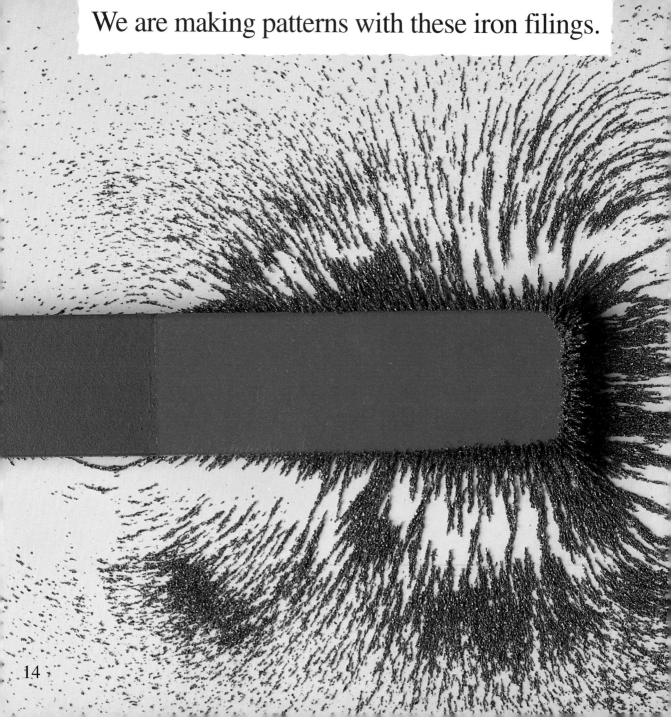

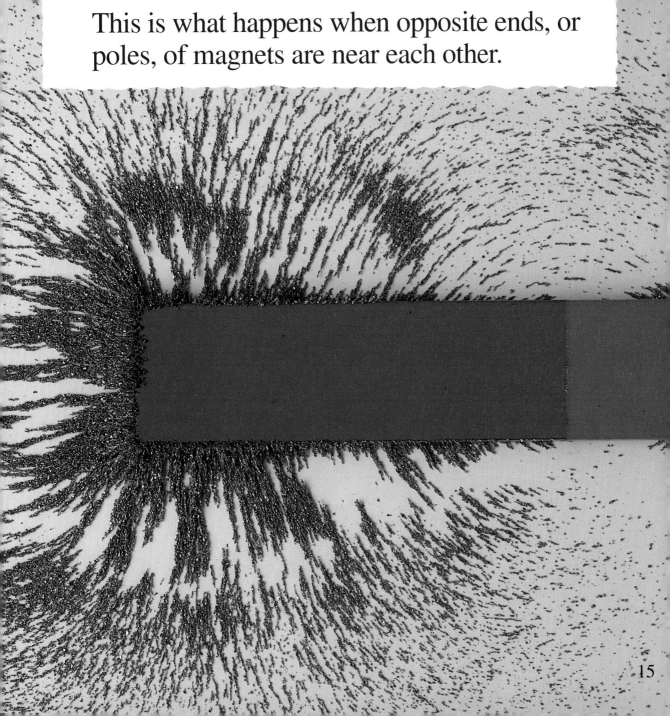

This is what happens when opposite ends, or poles, of magnets are near each other.

This is what happens when like ends, or poles, are near each other.

I can make these magnets float in the air.

My magnet moves this boat
along a paper bridge.

We are attaching our magnets to fishing poles.

My magnet lifts this car out of the water.

John can't lift the boat with his magnet.

My magnet will not pick up
gold treasure from the sand.

23

Which of these objects will stick to our magnets?

25

FOR MORE INFORMATION

Notes for Parents and Teachers

As you share this book with young readers, these notes may help you explain the scientific concepts behind the different activities.

pages 4, 5, 8, 9, 10, 12, 20, 24-25 Sticking power

Magnets mainly attract objects containing iron and steel — steel has iron in it. They also attract other metals, such as nickel and cobalt.

Magnets were first made more than two thousand years ago from a black rock called lodestone that has natural magnetic powers. The rock was discovered in a place called Magnesia, which is in modern-day Turkey. The word *magnet* comes from this ancient place name. The lodestone contains an iron ore called magnetite.

pages 6, 7 All sorts of magnets

Magnets come in different shapes — from bars and circles to horseshoes and cylinders. The shape of a magnet affects where the poles are.

pages 11, 20 How strong?

Magnets have different strengths that are not necessarily reflected in their size. Some small magnets can be quite powerful.

pages 12, 13, 14, 15, 16, 17 Pull and push

The pull of a magnet is strongest at certain points, which are called the magnetic poles. On a bar magnet, the poles are at either end of the magnet, and they behave differently from one another. They are sometimes colored red and blue or marked north and south. If you tie a thread around a bar magnet and let it swing freely, it will come to rest with one end pointing to the Earth's North Pole and one end pointing to the Earth's South Pole. This is because the Earth itself behaves as if it has a gigantic magnet along its center. The smaller magnets we use every day line up with the Earth's magnetic field. The easiest rule to remember about the poles of magnets is that *like poles repel and opposite poles attract.*

pages 14, 15, 16 Lines of force

The lines of force given off by magnets are invisible. But if iron filings are sprinkled around the magnets, they collect along these lines of force. More iron filings cluster together at the poles of the magnets where the force is strongest. Where the force is weaker, the lines are farther apart. The pictures of iron filings on these pages show that opposite poles attract each other and like poles repel each other.

pages 18, 20, 21
Stopping the force

Magnets will still attract objects through a barrier that does not contain iron as long as the barrier is not so thick that the object is beyond the reach of the magnetic field. The magnet on page 18 moves the boat along because it can still attract the metal paper clip under the boat through a thick paper bridge.

Things to Do

1. Go fish

Make a fishing game using a magnet, string, and metal paper clips. Cut out ten small fish shapes from construction paper, two each of different colors. Attach a paper clip to each "fish," then put the fish into a box. Tie a piece of string onto a magnet. Dangle the magnet into the box and try to "catch" matching fish. You can play this game alone or with a friend.

2. Magnet maze

Draw a maze or a wiggly path on a large piece of paper. Ask some friends to hold the paper in the air. Put a paper clip at the start of the maze and hold a magnet underneath the paper. Can you guide the paper clip through the maze without touching any lines?

3. Make a magnet

You can make a temporary magnet out of a metal paper clip or nail. Rub the paper clip or nail along the side of a magnet about fifty times. Be sure to rub along the magnet only in one direction. Will your new magnet pick up other paper clips or metal objects? How long does its magnetic power last?

4. Cork work

Have an adult help you push a thumb tack into the side of a cork. Put the cork into a sink or pan full of water and see if you can move it with a magnet. Then hang the cork from the edge of a table with a piece of string. Use your magnet to move the cork from side to side through the air.

Fun Facts about Magnets

1. Most magnets are made of three metals: iron, cobalt, and nickel. A combination of metals, as in a magnet, is called an alloy.

2. Doorbells, telephones, television sets, tape recorders, and computers all use magnets.

3. Everything that sticks to a magnet is metal, but not all metals stick to a magnet.

4. The heaviest magnet in the world is in the Joint Institute for Nuclear Research near Moscow. This enormous magnet weighs over 42,000 tons!

5. Some scientists believe birds use the Earth's magnetic field to help them navigate, or find their way, while migrating.

6. Country veterinarians sometimes use magnets to pick up pieces of wire or other metal from inside a cow's stomach.

7. If you cut a magnet in half, each of the two new magnets you create will have a north and south pole. No matter how many times the magnet is cut, each new piece will have a north and south pole.

8. The Earth itself is a big magnet, with north and south poles at opposite ends.

9. Chinese inventors made the first compasses thousands of years ago.

10. Doctors sometimes use magnets to remove tiny pieces of steel from workers' eyes.

Glossary

filings — small particles or fragments removed from a larger object by a file (a steel tool used for smoothing and shaping).

float — to rest or drift on top of a liquid or air.

horseshoes — U-shaped pieces of iron that are nailed to a horse's hoof.

iron — a strong, hard, silvery white or gray metal that can be magnetized.

objects — things that have a shape and can be seen and felt.

paper clips — small pieces of wire that are bent into curved shapes. Paper clips are used to hold loose sheets or pieces of paper together.

patterns — shapes or designs that can be used as models for making something.

poles — either ends of a magnet.

refrigerators — containers that keep food and other items cold.

sand — tiny pieces or grains of loose rock.

spoons — metal utensils used for eating and also for measuring.

stick — (v) to attach or fasten; to become attached to something, unable to move.

treasures — very valuable persons or objects.

Places to Visit

Everything we do involves some basic scientific principles. Listed below are a few museums that offer a variety of scientific information and experiences. You may also be able to locate other museums in your area. Just remember: you don't always have to visit a museum to experience the wonders of science. Science is everywhere!

Museum of Science and Industry
57th Street and Lake Shore Drive
Chicago, IL 60637

Ontario Science Center
770 Don Mills Road
Don Mills, Ontario
M3C 1T3

The Exploratorium
3601 Lyon Street
San Francisco, CA 94123

Science Center of British
    Columbia
1455 Quebec Street
Vancouver, British Columbia
V6A 3Z7

The Smithsonian Institution
1000 Jefferson Drive SW
Washington, D.C. 20560

More Books to Read

All About Magnets
    Stephen Krensky
    (Scholastic, Inc.)

Amazing Magnets
    David Adler
    (Troll Associates)

Experiments with Magnets
Helen Challand
(Childrens Press)

Science Book of Magnets
Neil Ardley
(Harcourt Brace)

My First Batteries and Magnet Book
(Dorling Kindersley)

Science with Magnets
Helen Edom
(Usborne Publishing)

Videotapes

Magnets (Coronet)
Magnets: The Dragon's Secret (Encyclopedia Britannica)

Magnets! Magnets! (Barr)
My First Science Video (Sony)

Index